Girl

1936 – 1937

Renee Essex-Crosby

## Contents

Introduction

THE DIARY  Waddow Hall 4$^{th}$-11$^{th}$ July 1936

Guide & Rangers in Norway 29$^{th}$ May to 12$^{th}$ June 1937
Camping in the 1930s
Epilogue
Copyright

# Introduction

This is a record of two Girl Guide Holidays taken by my Mother, the first in 1936 to Waddow Hall in Lancashire a Girl Guide Centre (as it still is today), the other to Norway in 1937, an adventurous undertaking for the time. She records her enjoyment of the packed programme of events at Waddow, and her first ride in a 'Diesel Car'. In Norway she encounters sometimes Spartan conditions among the glorious scenery where the party of blue-clad Guides find themselves the cynosure of all eyes. Then there is the Unfortunate Incident of the pudding...

She kept many photographs and postcards in her diary to complement her writing, these are included. Guiding clearly provided some independence and release from the constraints of Society at that time – before she married my father she was not left alone with him during his visits to the family home, not even for a goodbye kiss – and she was 32 by then!

I have also added a chapter on Girl Guide camping in the 1930s based on my Mother's verbal accounts and her photographs.

Mary Berry

*Renee in uniform*

# THE DIARY WADDOW HALL 4TH-11TH JULY 1936

The most enjoyable holiday I have ever had was at Waddow Hall during the above mentioned week. Waddow in Clitheroe is situated on the borders of Yorkshire and Lancashire; in fact the boundary line is the river Ribble which runs at the bottom of the grounds.

It was a most agreeable surprise to find instead of the large industrial town which I had visualised from the postal address of Clitheroe, Lancs that Clitheroe is a most beautiful spot on the banks of the river Ribble with the most beautiful (and historic) Pendle Hill only a couple of miles away to the South East and the wild and beautiful moors a few miles away to the north. Pendle Hill is well known in Lancashire as the hill on which in olden days the local witches were burnt. There are also the remains of Clitheroe castle near here, and just outside the grounds of Waddow is the historic Brungerley Bridge, where King Henry V1 was captured after the battle of Hexham.

One thing that strikes a visitor to Lancs from the South is the stone walls dividing the fields instead of hedges, and the stone houses. Also the plants and flowers seem late in blossoming compared with the South. Waddow Hall itself is a very old house,

dating from the $12^{th}$ century and in the grounds is an ancient headless statue the origin and meaning of which no one quite knows. The grounds are very beautiful, most of it being used as camp sites and pasture land, and there is also a large and well-kept garden with, among a very large variety of trees, two very beautiful and ancient copper beech trees.

There is also a tennis court, but unfortunately it was too wet during the week for us to be able to play. The house inside is most beautiful and really "Guidey". The rooms are beautifully furnished and are named after the people, country or district that furnished them. I myself slept in "Blackpool" a sweet little room in mauve. Everything in Waddow has been given by somebody, and we were shown several of Princess Mary's lovely gifts to Waddow. What strikes one so immediately on entering Waddow is the peaceful, happy "Guidey" atmosphere. Although I went to Waddow all alone, I felt at home immediately I got there and had a thoroughly enjoyable time.

There were only 11 other Rangers staying the week, so I soon got to know them all. Two of the Rangers were foreign girls, one from Sweden and one from Malay. They were very nice indeed and it was very interesting meeting them. We were divided into two patrols – The Plovers and Herons. I was in the Plover Patrol, of which I was P.L. for half the week, and was so fortunate as to have both the foreign Rangers in my patrol. I now know the Swedish for Be Prepared – "Var Redo". We had Ranger training sessions in the morning and the rest of the day we were free. We usually ended up with camp fires in the evening. We had very little orderly work to do, practically everything being done by the staff of maids who are all Rangers, Guiders, or Guides.

I also quite enjoyed the journey to Waddow. At Euston Stn. two ladies got into my carriage and after a while we got talking and I discovered that one of them had a daughter in the Guide Movement and the other knew a Past Ranger, so we had quite a lot in common to talk about. I changed at Preston and while having a cup of tea in the refreshment room, a lady came up to me and said "Are you a Guide – I have a daughter in the Guide Movement". We then started talking and I found she had lived in Lancashire for many years, and knew Waddow quite well, in fact she knew the previous owners! She proceeded to tell me quite a lot about local history, pointing out places of interest from the train window, and as she was also travelling to Clitheroe Stn. I had quite an interesting time. Guide uniform certainly is a sign of friendship. I have often noticed how many people will talk to you if you are in uniform. If I had been in mufti probably

I should have had quite a lonely journey.

Below is the programme of our activities during the week:-

<u>Sunday</u> Every morning before breakfast we had colours and prayers and after breakfast on Sunday some of us went to Waddington Church. In the afternoon we had a house tour, when we were shown all over the house and grounds, and in the evening we had a Guides Own.

<u>Monday</u> We began Monday in fine style with a fire alarm!! We had been previously warned that sometime during the week we should have a fire alarm and just after the rising bell had gone at 7.30 a.m. on Monday, the fire alarm went. Luckily I had got up early and was completely dressed, but one Ranger was still in bed and one was just about to have a bath when it went! My. What a scramble first thing in the morning! Still we all got out of the house in record time. We began the morning session with a nature game (initial letters). We then had a tree competition, followed by a discussion and practice about clouds and wind. In the afternoon 6 of us went to Blackpool, arriving home about 10p.m. unfortunately too late for the camp fire.

On our way back from Blackpool we had our first ride in a Diesel Car. This is not a real thoroughbred train, but a strange mixture of train, trolley bus and ordinary single decker bus. We entered this Diesel Car at Blackburn and for the rest of the journey to Clitheroe Station had a most amusing time. The Diesel Car runs along the ordinary railway track, but is a small car about the size of a single –decker bus, and has windows both at the back and front as well as at the sides. The passengers can sit in front on a level with the driver, and it is most strange to be able to see the railway lines in front of you all the time, and to be able to see the end of a tunnel when just entering it. The conductor (it has a conductor who shuts the doors after the passengers have boarded it, and then rings a bell for the driver to start) was most amused at our remarks, and as we had in our haversacks the remains of our lunch which we could not eat, we proceeded to feed the conductor and driver who seemed most grateful. I am sure the conductor must have been a scout at some time or other as he always shared whatever we gave him with his mate, the driver. We were all very sorry when at last we reached Clitheroe Stn. After our most amusing journey and as a memento the conductor presented us all with a timetable! I don't think any of us will forget our first ride in a Diesel Car!

*1936 Timetable - Diesel Car one Class only*

Please retain for reference.

**RAIL SERVICE.**

## CLITHEROE & BLACKBURN

Calling at intermediate Stations
6th JULY to 27th SEPTEMBER inclusive, 1936.

| From CLITHEROE. | | From BLACKBURN. | |
|---|---|---|---|
| a.m. | p.m. | a.m. | p.m. |
| 7 0 | 6 15A | 6 3 | 5 39 |
| 7 34 | 6*35 | 6 55 | 6* 2 |
| 8 7 | 6 49 | 8 16 | 6 33SX |
| 9 0 | 7 46 | 9* 0 | 6 51SO |
| 9*30 | 8*20SX | 9*28 | 7*11 |
| 9 55 | 8 31SO | 9 43SO | 7 31 |
| 10*35 | 8*35SO | 9 46SX | 8*13 |
| 11*25 | 9 16 | 10 3F | 8 40 |
| 11 42SO | 9*35 | 10E10SO | 9 15 |
| 11 44SX | 10 19 | 10E15SX | 9*48SX |
|  | 10*30SX | 10*45 | 10 15SO |
| p.m. | 11 10SO | 11 40 | 10 38 |
| 12 27 |  | p.m. | 11 16SX |
| 1* 0 | Sundays | 12* 5 | 11 30SO |
| 1 29 | a.m. | 12 27 | Sundays |
| 2* 2SX | 7 49 | 12*40SX | a.m. |
| 2*16SO | 11 3 | 1 2SX | 9 17 |
| 2 53E |  | 1*10SO | 10 15 |
| 3 16 | p.m. | 1 24SO | p.m. |
| 3*35 | 1 21 | 2 11 | 12 10 |
| 3*50SO | 3 26 | 2 45SO | 2 15 |
| 4* 0SX | 4 39 | 2*50 | 2 40 |
| 4 38 | 6 21 | 3*19 | 3 10 |
| 5 5C | 8 22 | 3 55B | 4 30 |
| 5*18 | 8 54 | 4*15 | 5 15D |
| 5 29 | 9 49 | 4 27 | 6 55 |
| 5*54 | 10 22 | 4 43A | 8 30 |
|  |  | 5*15 | 9 30 |

*—Leyland-Diesel Rail Car (one class only).
A—Tues. and Fris. only. B—Whalley and Clitheroe only.
C—Whalley and Blackburn only. Also to Langho on Saturdays. D—Not to Langho. E—Express.
F—Sats. only. Will not run after August 29th—Express.
SO—Saturdays only. SX—Saturdays excepted.

SEE PAGE 10.

Tuesday  At 7.30a.m. Four of us (including the two foreign Rangers) set off for the Lake District. We went to Lake Windermere which we crossed by steamer, and alighted at Ambleside where we ate our dinner, and then we walked to Rydal Water and Grasmere, where we saw Wordsworth's Cottage, by which time it was time for us to return to the station. We were very fortunate in having a glorious day, and although we were all rather weary by the time we arrived back at 11p.m., we all agreed it had been a most marvellous day. It was our first visit to the Lake District and I am sure we shall none of us forget the marvellous scenery we saw.

WE HIKED TO HERE.

Dove Cottage Wordsworth's House

Wednesday  At the beginning of the session on Wednesday morning we had a most thrilling game.

We found a message in the hall that the famous Waddow diamonds had been stolen! After a while we found a clue which enabled us to catch just in time a message in Morse being given by an accomplice to the thief on the river bank. Of course everyone dashed down to the river to capture the thief, which was done after a great struggle – and my word he (or rather she) <u>could</u> struggle. After tying up the thief we discovered that the accomplice had managed to get the diamonds and was rowing across the river with them in a boat. One of the Rangers immediately plunged in (fully dressed) after the accomplice (who by the way was the Guider in charge) and after a struggle we managed to get possession of the lost jewels. While we were all tidying ourselves on the bank and saying what fun it had been, one of the Rangers put the finishing touch to things by accidentally slipping and falling backwards into the water! The hot water pipes in the drying room certainly came in useful that morning!

For the rest of the session we had competitions on hiding ourselves both with and without cover, and also hiding large objects. We also had a most helpful discussion on the Ranger Star test and Guide Law. The afternoon we spent in walking about by the river. It was after having managed to ford the river by means of submerged natural stepping stones that we had discovered during the afternoon, that I and two other Rangers became smitten with a desire to compose poetry! The following was the result of our combined efforts! We are still trying to think of a tune to sing it to:-

> We three Rangers from Waddow Hall,
>
> Sat beside a waterfall,
>
> As we did paddle, we did fall, which did make us shout and call, -
>
> To Waddow Hall.

WE CROSSED THESE STEPPING STONES.

This verse is quite true, as we did nearly slip into the river when fording it. The waterfall refers to the weir! In the evening we challenged the staff to Sports and just managed to win by 1 point. We ended the evening with a camp fire.

<u>Thursday</u> We commenced the morning session by having a colour practice as some of us were none too sure of it. We then had country dancing and we also learnt a most fascinating sword dance. We also did some plaster casts during the morning and played a very thrilling stalking game (hidden necklaces). In the afternoon we attempted to climb Pendle Hill, but as a storm started before we got very far, we had to return to Waddow. We had a camp fire again in the evening.

<u>Friday</u> We spent most of the morning session by going out and planning a camp site. The rest of the morning we spent in emergency practices. From these emergencies we learnt the right way to climb a ladder and rescue a cat, how to improvise a stretcher and carry a person whose back is injured, and what to do if lost in a forest. As it was very wet in the afternoon we stayed indoors. In the evening as it was still wet we had a fire lit in the drawing room and had a camp fire in there.

Saturday Spent the first part of the morning packing and practising sword and country dancing, and then went for a last walk along the river bank (in the pouring rain) and then after an uneventful journey arrived back home again, firmly resolved to visit Waddow again next year.

In fact she never did return to Waddow- but having experienced the Lake District returned for many happy Walking and Youth Hostelling holidays with colleagues from County Hall during the Second World War.

Renee Essex-Crosby

Guide Lieutenant & Ranger P.L.   later Guide Captain

1$^{St}$ Long Ditton (St Mary's) Esher Dis. Kingston Div.

"The Old Harrow"Weston
GreenThames DittonSurrey

<u>WADDOW</u>

## Ranger Conference and Holiday Week July 4th – 11th 1936

| | |
|---|---|
| Guider in Charge | Miss Newnham |
| Secretary | Miss Anderdon |
| Housekeeper | Miss Nicholson |

# GUIDE & RANGERS IN NORWAY 29TH MAY TO 12TH JUNE 1937

| | |
|---|---:|
| Guider in Charge<br>Beer (District Comm for Southall) | Mrs |
| Assistant Commandant<br>Ford | Miss |
| Head of my Group (Yellow)<br>Windsor | Miss |

Having read the most fascinating accounts of Norway in the "Guide" I decided to be more adventurous this year and spend a fortnight in Norway. It was certainly the most unusual and thrilling holiday I have had! There were

54 of us in all, of varying ages from 14 to 40. We were divided into 6 groups, each group having a different colour and having a Guider in charge of it.

At 11a.m. on Saturday 29th May about 30 of our party met at King's Cross Station to commence our long journey. It was a lovely hot sunny day and proved to be the forerunner of a fortnight's heat wave in England. Unfortunately we saw very little of the sun in Norway, the weather there being mostly wet and cold, with the exception of 3 or 4 days when the sun actually did shine! At midday the train started for Newcastle where we were to pick up the rest of our party and board the "Venus" en route for Bergen, Norway. After 6 hours comfortable (?) journey in the stiflingly hot train (most of the windows refusing to open) we at last arrived at Newcastle and boarded the "Venus". For many of us this was a great thrill as some of us had never been on a boat before for any length of time.

We had supper shortly after going aboard (taking up the whole of the ship's dining room) and then wandered about the ship exploring our quarters, watching all the luggage being swung aboard by cranes and the sailors getting ready to 'let go the anchor'. By this time we had all managed to introduce ourselves to each other. Being such a large party it took us some time to remember everybody's name correctly.

I think the sailors and other passengers were very amused to see such a horde of blue-clad figures wandering about, but by the time we got back to England we had got quite hardened to being stared at! We all stood on the deck waving goodbye to England which rapidly got further and further away from us. When at last we reached the mouth of the Tyne we really felt we were on the way to Norway. Most of us stood for some time by the deck rails watching the glorious sunset over the sea and striving to hide the strange feelings we soon began to experience. Alas, one by one we hastily disappeared below deck! – A few of us to be seen no more until Norway was reached. Why must ships go up and down and then roll from side to side! The voyage would have been so much pleasanter if only the ship had kept still!! We were on the sea for 20 hours, and never have I longed so much for a day to end! Each hour seemed like two! However by 3p.m. the next afternoon we were in the Norwegian Fjords, and as things felt a little steadier by then, I endeavoured to get off my bunk. In scrambling down I knocked my funny-bone and the next thing I knew someone was bringing me round after a faint! Apparently I nearly knocked one of my cabin-mates over in my disgraceful performance.

Was I glad to see Norway! The dry land (although

it was raining hard) looked so lovely after seeing (or rather feeling) nothing but sea for 20 hours. Waiting to greet us at the Quayside were some Norwegian Girl Guides who assisted us through the Customs and then took us to our rooms at the Hotel Bibelskuleheimen, Bergen, where we were greeted with a quite English meal of fried eggs.

NORSK SPEIDERPIKEFORBUND

The food in Norway is quite nice – they seem particularly fond of horsd' oeuvres and highly seasoned dishes. The bread, milk and cheese are slightly different to the English. The cheese in particular is most extraordinary - it <u>looks</u> just like carbolic soap and tastes just like <u>fudge</u>! However while in Norway we just eat what was given us and hoped for the best! Norwegians seem to economise on cutlery and plates. At nearly every meal we only had one knife for all courses and one plate for all courses. We got so used to this by the end of our holiday, that we were afraid we should start doing the same when we arrived at home, much to our families' horror! However we managed to restrain ourselves when we arrived home! The people of Norway are very friendly, although not many of them can speak English, and as none of us could speak Norwegian, we had some very amusing times.

Apparently the Norwegians had never seen so many queer-looking Girl Guides before – whenever they saw any of us they just stared and stared!! Norway is a most marvellous country for scenery- awfully wild and untouched with tremendous snow-capped mountains, waterfalls and wonderful fjords everywhere – with just here and there a tiny village with simple wooden houses. Everything in the little Norwegian villages we went to was very simple but spotlessly clean – most houses have electric light or else candles.

They do not seem to use gas much in Norway – even the cooking they do on big stoves using wood for fuel. The people's ordinary dress is not so very different from ours, except that the small boys all wear thick stockings or plus-fours. The women only wear their most attractive and beautifully decorated national costumes on special occasions, such as at the yearly confirmation service, which we were fortunate enough to see one Sunday at Eidford. Most of the roads up the mountains are marvellous work – hairpin bends every other minute, tunnels and avalanche protection covers all along the narrow road. It was quite a thrill to go for a car ride – especially when one met something coming in the opposite direction. Apparently in Norway one can't go out of sight of a mountain. Surrey seems horribly flat after it all.

PAGE 23.

The flowers, plants and trees of Norway are very similar to those in England, birch and fir predominating among the trees, especially on the mountains, where the rather severe climate seems to stunt their growth a great deal. The plant life seems to be about a month behind England. The evenings in Norway are remarkably light – in fact it never seems to get dark art all! I understand we were quite near 'the land of the midnight sun'. It seemed awfully strange to wake up at 2 or 3 o'clock at night and find it comparatively light. Many of the houses in Norway have double windows – on account of the snow in winter we were told. Straw is used quite a lot in Norway for mattresses, and in all the fields we saw short fences dotted about ready to dry the straw on when cut. We were quite mystified at first by these little fences all over the place, until we found out the reason for them.

The foreign money was also great fun. We felt quite good mathematicians by the time by had finished calculating in wirs, half kroners and kroners.

We arrived at our hotel in Bergen about 6p.m. on Sunday, and after having a meal and unpacking we all felt ready for bed – having been travelling since midday on Saturday.

<u>Monday</u> After breakfast our first thought was to change our English money and obtain some postcards and stamps. It was certainly a most amusing business! We managed to discover a Bank and then all trooped in much to the surprise of everybody outside and inside the Bank, and proceeded to wave bank-notes in front of the poor bank clerks. Apparently they understood us for they gave us a

weird collection of wirs, kroners and notes for our money. We spent quite a comical few minutes examining and trying to calculate our new money – much to the Bank's amusement. We then managed to discover a post-office, and after some difficulty managed to find out what stamps we needed for out post-cards and letters. We then trooped out of the post-office (much to the clerk's relief I believe) and proceeded to make our first efforts at shopping in a foreign country.

What fun! We pointed to things, held up our fingers, gesticulated and in the end usually managed to get what we wanted. By the end of the holiday we all thought we should be doing the same in London! We found the traffic too, most confusing – everything happening to the right instead of the left! However none of us got run over. In the afternoon we went up a mountain called Florien, by railway. When we arrived at the top we found we had a most marvellous view of Bergen. After wandering about the mountain paths for a while admiring the marvellous scenery all around we went to the café which was at the top of the mountain for tea. It was at this café we had our first glimpse of the women's national dress – as all the waitresses were dressed in the national costume. We then returned to our Hotel for supper.

<u>Tuesday</u>   Spent the morning shopping. Got quite expert at making ourselves understood by

gesticulating. It started to rain when we first left the Hotel and as the time passed it just rained harder and harder! Bergen is said to be the wettest place in Norway – it rains 360 days a year and the other few days are not quite dry – I can quite believe it! Ended up the morning by having a cup of coffee & biscuits in a café - where a kind Norwegian gentleman had to assist us in making ourselves understood. After lunch we went for a car-ride along the fjords and saw some very interesting ruins of an ancient monastery. We also went inside one the oldest Norwegian churches – a very quaint looking building of wonderfully carved wood. In the evening we had a camp-fire sing-song in the dining room of our Hotel with some of the Norwegian Guides. We thoroughly enjoyed their singing – and they appeared to do ours!

<u>Wednesday</u> At 9 a.m. we started by car on a 5 hour run to Oystese, our next stopping place. During this car-ride we saw some of the most awe-inspiring scenery in Norway. One minute we were high up a mountain on a narrow road cut out of the rock, going through tunnels and having hair-pin bends, with the river looking a mere white streak many hundreds of feet below us, and the next we were whizzing along by the side of the rushing, marvellously clear river. We saw many wonderful waterfalls during our ride and our driver obligingly stopped at one so we could take a snap of it. On arrival at Oystese we found the sun actually beginning to shine! After having our dinner we spent the rest of the day exploring our surroundings. Oystese is a beautiful little village on the side of the Hardanger Fjord, surrounded by mountains and with a lovely view of a glacier! While here we first saw carts drawn by horses with their little foals running along by the side of them. They were a very popular subject for snaps!

PAGE 29/30.

At Oystese we stayed at a Youth Hostel at least most of us did – being such a large party we took up all the accommodation at the Hostel and a few of our party had to stay at a farm-house nearby, while 7 of us (myself included) had to sleep on straw paillasses in the mangle-room! We were highly amused and from thenceforward we were known as 'the mangle-room people'.

Thursday  On Thursday we had a positive heat-wave, so we just spent the day strolling about and sun-bathing. Unfortunately one of our party now developed tonsillitis and had to remain here for a whole week.

Friday On Friday afternoon we left by steamer for Eidford. After a very pleasant 4 hours journey through wonderful scenery we arrived at Eidford where nearly the whole village turned out to have a look at us! Eidford we discovered was a charming little village in a hollow at the bottom of the mountains on the Hardanger Fjord. Here the snow on the mountains seemed to have lingered longest and in some places we were quite close to the snow. Here the sun deserted us again and once more mackintoshes had to be donned. The youth hostel here was quite small, so various parties had to sleep out elsewhere – some at the Post Office and others in nearby cottages. It was here I had the luxury of a room to myself and also a whole wash basin and jug to myself!! Up to the present we had slept at least 7 in a room with only one wash basin between us. Here we also had to get our own washing water from the crystal-clear rushing mountain river at the back of the Hostel. It was quite a skilful job to get a jug of water without sitting down in the river – and it was so horribly cold too! However we all managed to keep out of the water!

*Renee the author fetching water*

<u>Saturday</u> As it was still raining on Saturday morning most of us went for a coach ride to Odda – a small town some miles away. It was a very pretty drive, and in one part we passed several miles of cherry trees, covered with most appetising-looking cherries. On arrival at Odda we got out of the coach and proceeded to ask the driver at what time we should meet him again for our return journey. We then discovered that he could not speak English, and as we could not speak Norwegian, we were in rather a dilemma. However eventually we managed to find someone who could speak English and act as our interpreter! We entered a Hotel while in Odda and while drinking our coffee a girl entered and gave us the half salute. We then of course tried to welcome her, but as neither could speak the others language we had to greet each other by signs – anyway we could all give the Guide salute and hand-shake & guide smile! Mrs Beer then discovered that the Norwegian girl could speak German, so they both started talking away to each other in German, while we just looked on.

On the journey back we noticed that a number of the cows had bells on their necks and that several people were wearing clogs. At supper that night we had a most amusing episode. We were given a most delicious pudding and after everyone had had a helping there was quite a goodly portion left and everyone was hoping for a second helping. The pudding was passed round to my friend Agnes who as it happened did not want any more – she was just going to pass it on when it all slipped off the dias and landed on her plate! – Much to her horror and our amusement. Of course everyone teased Agnes about her greediness, and after that, pudding was a sore subject with Agnes. In the evening three Y.W.C.A. Norwegian Guides arrived to stay the night with us.

*Youth Hostel*

<u>Sunday</u>   On Sunday morning we were delighted to hear that there was to be a Confirmation Service at Eidford Church. This was a very small, simple little Church, with no organ or other music, the congregation just singing on their own. Confirmation Services are apparently a great event

– all the people from nearby villages coming to the service. At the confirmation service all the women and little girls appear in their most attractive national costume. We of course all wanted to photograph them and they did not appear to mind at all, but most obligingly posed for us.

In the afternoon we went for a car-ride to see

Norway's biggest waterfall. It certainly took our breath away when we saw it! While on this drive we also went up a mountain and on a plateau near the top we saw our first <u>wild</u> reindeer. Great was our excitement at the sight of a wild reindeer trotting through the snow. This was the first time we had actually been within touching distance of the snow, so our driver kindly stopped the coach and we all dashed out and had a snowball fight! On a summer holiday imagine! It all seemed awfully unreal somehow to be up there walking on the snow on a wild desolate mountain plateau. After a while we were quite glad to get into our coaches again and snuggle down among nice warm rugs!

<u>Monday</u>  On Monday we had breakfast at <u>6a.m</u>. – what groans there were when this was announced the previous night - as we were starting at 7a.m. for Myrdal our next stopping place. At 7 a.m. we boarded two small steamers as the start of our long, varied and interesting journey to Myrdal – an Hotel 3,000 ft up a mountain! The skipper of our steamer had most thoughtfully hoisted a minute Union Jack, so that we could "sail under the English Flag" as he said. After 4 hrs journey on the Fjord we disembarked and got into cars for an hour's drive to the railway station.

As we were rather late in landing, and as the trains only go twice a day our drivers had to "step on it" to get us to the station in time. Of course one of the cars would break down on the way and in the consequent scramble one of the girls had her hand crushed rather badly. However it was practically better by the time we left Norway. Eventually we arrived at the Station without any more mishaps and just managed to catch our train!

After a short train journey we at length arrived at Myrdal – which consists of one large hotel and about half a doz. small houses. Myrdal Hotel is situated over 3,000 ft up a mountain, with a marvellous waterfall and lake just below it. Here the snow was still on most of the ground, in many places 6ft deep. At Myrdal the sun again favoured us, and we felt quite hot at times – although walking on snow! The hotel was a very large one so here we were not the only guests. As it was however we took up most of the lounge and drawing room and I think we gave the other guests quite a shock at first when they saw us all marching in! After having our lunch we spent the rest of the day walking about the mountain paths.

<u>Tuesday</u>  In the morning we all went for a hike to the Flam Valley – a most beautiful valley at the bottom of the mountain. We descended to the valley moderately easily by means of zig-zag paths, but my goodness what a stiff climb up we found it! When we all did eventually arrive back at the hotel we just sat and panted! – But the view was most certainly worth the climb. As the afternoon turned out to be rather wet, we spent the rest of the time in the hotel lounge reading.

US EXPLORING NORWAY.

<u>Wednesday</u>  Spent the morning have a last walk about the mountain. After lunch we all went to the Station where after a long wait in a very cool wind,

we at last boarded the train en route for Bergen again. The Norwegian trains are unfortunately not nearly so comfortable as English trains – the seats being just bare boards with no trace of padding. After 4 hrs travel in such a train we were quite glad to reach Bergen again.

On arrival at Bergen Station we found the station absolutely packed. Apparently on our train there were also a party of Russian Students, and the whole of Bergen (a very large town) seemed to have turned out to meet them. After the crowds cheering had died down and the students had started to move away, the crowd suddenly spotted our party and apparently thought we were part of the entertainment, for they started to swarm round us, staring and talking hard! However, seeing we did nothing spectacular, they at last dispersed and we were able to continue on our way to our hotel!

<u>Thursday</u>  After packing we spent the morning having a last walk round the parks in Bergen and taking our last look at Norway's marvellous mountains and hearing for the last time the strange Norwegian language. After such a marvellous fortnight we were very loath indeed to leave Norway. At 11 a.m. we once more boarded the "Venus" (with many qualms on my part) and after waving goodbye to the Norwegian Guides who had come to see us off, we felt the engines begin to throb under us

and knew we were at last on our way back to dear old England. Fortunately the sea was much calmer coming back, and I had a comparatively pleasant voyage to Newcastle.

4675 Bergen. Fantoft stavkirke.

Friday morning we were all on deck very early, all striving to be the first to sight land. About 8 a.m. we saw land – ENGLAND. Great was our excitement, although it was only the extremely flat and uninteresting- looking Newcastle-on-Tyne. We disembarked about 9 a.m. in brilliant sunshine and after going through the Customs (who passed most of our cases through without looking at them) we boarded a train for Kings Cross.

As we were such a large party the railway had to provide an extra lunch for us in the restaurant car, much to the disgust of the other passengers who had to wait until we had finished. As we proceeded to Kings Cross we gradually dropped members of our party at various stations, and many were the good-byes said during the journey. At 5.30 p.m. we said a final farewell and thank you to Mrs Beer and then all scattered in various directions home – all agreeing that it had been a simply marvellous holiday, and vowing to meet again one day! I then made my way to Waterloo Station, and on walking across the platform was most agreeably surprised by a complete stranger giving me a real Guide smile and the half salute – a really Guidey welcome home to England after a Guide holiday abroad!

Post script

Alas! On 1st September 1939 England was at war with Germany, and the 2nd World War had started!

Eventually the Government asked those who had maps or snaps of Norway to let the British Army have them to help them in their efforts to free our Norwegian friends from the German grip on their country. This accounts for the gaps at the end of this book.

# CAMPING IN THE 1930S

This was very exciting in those days for Girl Guides and Rangers – a chance to something completely different and an escape from sometimes rather suffocating family life!

*Off to Camp, outside the 'Harrow', Renee standing left*

Renee lived in the old Harrow public house between Weston Green and Thames Ditton. Her father was the Landlord and her mother was equally involved in the running of it, with some support from Renee's sister who at 30 was nine years older and a confirmed spinster, or so they thought (decades later she astonished everyone by suddenly marrying in 1969 at the age of 65).

The car was arranged with the help of her father, a ride in a motor vehicle itself being an exciting experience for some of her young Guides.

*The Patrol with their kit   Renee standing on the left*

Equipment was naturally nothing like modern camping basics, tents were not even completely waterproof, I remember Mother saying how, if you merely brushed the inside of the tent after rain, water leaked through, and of course in the confines of a crowded space someone always *did* manage to do this.

*The Happy Campers! Renee middle back row*

The camping ground had to be inspected carefully – no pitching of tents under ash trees (which are prone to drop branches suddenly) – or indeed under any dangerous limbs. All excellent advice today too, as was the requirement to keep the camp site tidy. Even the turf, cut when the latrine pit was dug, was carefully kept to one side and watered daily, to be replaced when the pit was filled in on breaking camp.

# CAMPING IN THE 1930S

*Erecting the screens*

*The Camp Flagpole*

The Flagpole was the focal gathering point of the camp, and it was of course vital to hoist it the correct way up. Mother recalled her mortification when Guides she had entrusted with the task (who had assured her they knew what they were doing) proceeded to raise it upside down in front of some important visitors.

*Camp chores*

*Busy in camp*

One night, despite their best efforts the Guides' tents suffered badly in gale force wind and rain, so the occupants decamped to the driest shelter they could find until morning – the portico of a nearby mansion.

That morning the Butler opened the door to the sight of bedraggled Girl Guides sitting on the steps. "Would you care for some tea"? he enquired, as if this was a normal part of his duties. Mother thought this overwhelmingly kind, I felt he could at least have invited them all in to dry off – but this was after all the 1930s.

*Out with Wheelchair-bound fellow Guides*

Sometimes the Patrol helped take a group of handicapped Guides out for a day. The wheelchairs were incredibly heavy and difficult to manoeuvre mother recalled, and the forest location pictured here suggests an ambitious choice of destination.

***21st Birthday Party for poor girls!***

Finally, though not strictly a Guiding activity, my mother invited a group of "Slum Children" from London to celebrate her coming of age on 16th July

1934. This was something the better off did in those days, and with a spacious garden and open countryside around her home was an ideal location. Her elder sister Phyllis disliked this invasion and complained about the extra work it made to me years later, though it is very doubtful that my Aunt was of the least practical help.

# EPILOGUE

Norway was the end of her Diary keeping, during the Second World War she undertook secretarial work at Surrey County Hall and Fire Watch duties in her spare time but left no record of this, unlike her fiancé John Harris my Father. His diary follows - covering the dramatic events in the years 1942-44 when he served with the Eighth Army in Africa including the battle of El Alamein when he casually records 'flames and bombs being dropped near us'. He noted everyday life too, sometimes with a lack of political correctness as in 'gave the Wogs 2 tins of bully for 4 eggs – was it good to have a fry up of eggs and fried bread'.

Renee died in 2006 after a long widowhood of 26 years.

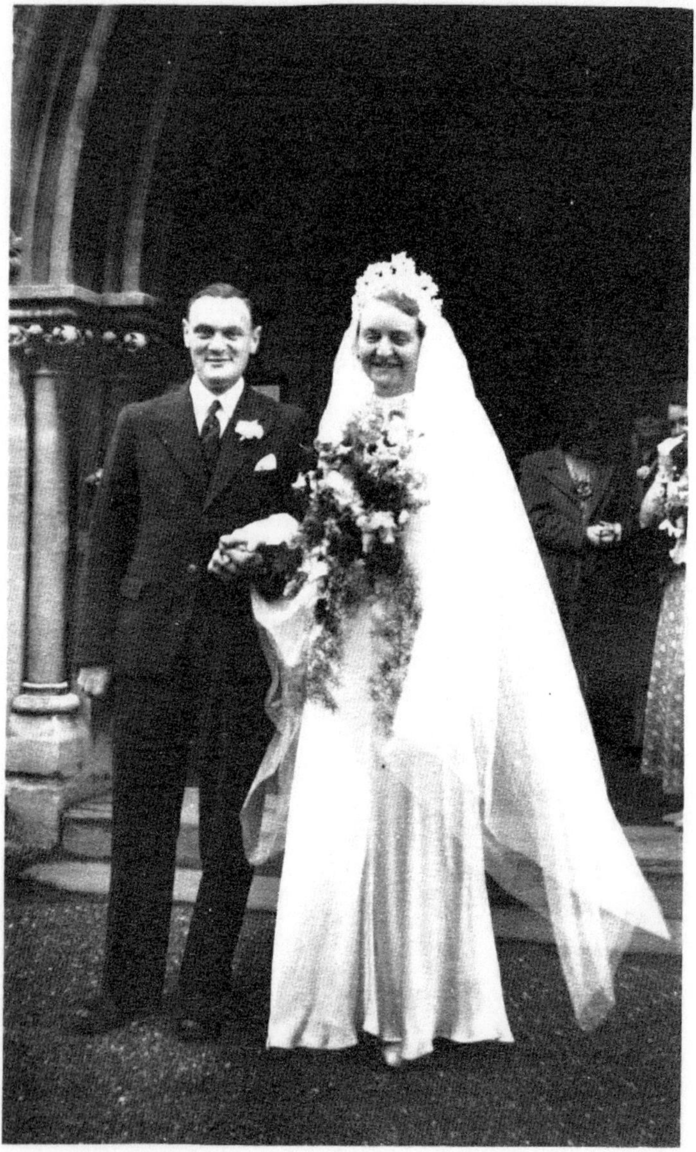

EPILOGUE

# My Mother's Guiding Days ended after her Wedding in 1946

**The Diary**

# COPYRIGHT

**Belongs to**

**Mary Berry**

**2012**

Printed by Amazon Italia Logistica S.r.l.
Torrazza Piemonte (TO), Italy